The Dark Side of Karate

Les Bubka

Copyright ©2021 Leszek Bubka.

All rights reserved. No part of this book may be used or reproduced by any means, graphic, electronic, or mechanical, including photocopying, recording, taping or by any information storage retrieval system without written permission of the author except in the case of brief quotations embodied in critical articles and reviews.

This book is a work of non-fiction. Unless otherwise stated, the author makes no explicit guarantees as to the accuracy of the information contained in this book.

Because of the dynamic nature of the Internet, any web addresses or links contained in this book may have changed since publication and may no longer be valid.

The author of this book does not dispense medical advice or prescribe the use of any technique as a form of treatment for physical, mental, emotional or medical problems without the advice of a physician. The intent of the author is only to offer information of a general nature to help you understand his journey. In the event you use any of the information in this book for yourself, which is your constitutional right, the author assumes no responsibility for your actions.

Foreword

"I'm no prophet. My job is making windows where there were once walls."

— Michel Foucault

A well-known assertion within anthropology is that traditions must be reimagined and repurposed for succeeding generations to remain relevant and vibrant. The task of reinvigorating tradition falls to innovators. Often derided during their lifetime in time, their adjustments and insights prove correct and necessary. Every field of human endeavour has such innovators. These innovators question and usually dare to identify current limitations, fallacies, or sometimes outright lies that manipulate and control tradition.

In the hands of those who control, traditions are often used to control and manipulate followers. Thus it often befalls the innovator to identify and name the manipulation and call out the emperor's new clothes. Martial arts, and in particular Karate, is rife with such manipulation. Cults of personality, tribalism, do as I say - not as I do are far too often par for those on the path of Karate. Thankfully the book you have in your hands begins a process of shining light into the dark side of Karate. It is the first step: A necessary step. This book traces one man's journey through the maelstrom and his emergence on the other side - worn, battered but full of energy, hope and empathy. Following the central tenet of Karate pioneer Kyan Chotoku, Karate has made Les` life and those around him better.

I first became interested in Les' work several years ago as he took up the mantle of innovator and saw the possibility for Karate to improve mental health. Already a trained coach and paramedic, Les could have simply begun yet another organisation. Indeed his pedigree in wrestling and Karate would have enabled such a step. However, in his typical and unassuming way, Les saw further than most of us and began to study mental health and well-being. More importantly, drawing upon personal experience, he reached out to folks often forgotten by the Karate world. He became a voice of reason, hope, and inclusion. I am in awe of his insights and energy. From running a Karate organisation to finding funding to authoring books and presenting his ever-popular podcast, Les Bubka is a necessary renaissance man within the field of martial arts. He reminds us that there is more to life than making money and achieving rank - there is the profound and rewarding commitment we have to each other.

In the current volume, Les brings his insight and energy into examining the underbelly of Karate, especially its culture, practices, and manipulation of tradition. Herein Les lays bare Karate's scams, liars, and ego driven manipulations. Les shares how organisations demanded and expected him to promote their agenda but only among those they deemed acceptable. Likewise, he sheds light on the darkness of insufferable myopia that many Karate organisations have and the vengeance they seek upon those who were once part of their sacred flock. Karate in this book smells of death - its lack of honour.

Dr. James Hach Sensei

Contents

Foreword iii
Contents vi
Introduction 1
Chapter 1 - The Old Master 3
Chapter 2 - Baptism of Fire...8
Chapter 3 - Games..13

    Choosing the Competition for Influence 15
    More Prestige 16
    Creation 16

Chapter 4 - Master of Puppets 18
Chapter 5 - Fear of the...22
Chapter 6 - Bribery 27

    Snatching Students 29
    Cajoling Coaches 31

Chapter 7 - Good Times..34
Chapter 8 - Ubiquitous Shitstorm.............................40
Chapter 9 - Demolition Man.....................................44
Chapter 10 - Search for Independence 49
Chapter 11 - Your Way or the Highway....................53

    Have Courage 54
    Be Committed 54
    Work Hard 55
    Be Honest 55

Use Your Initiative	*55*
Be Kind	*56*
Provide Leadership	*56*
Think Positively	*57*
Have Respect	*57*
Be Tolerant	*58*
Be Resilient	*58*

Chapter 12 - Everybody Lies	60
Chapter 13 - Allies	63
Summary	67
About the Author	73
Ready more by Les Bubka	74

Anxious Black Belt	*74*
Thoughts On Karate: A Collection of Articles	*74*
Rules for Success in Karate	*75*
Karate Journal	*75*

Introduction

Most of us Karate folk are proud of what we do, and always promote the positive side of the art. As with everything in life there are always two sides to the story. The positive and the negative, the light and the darkness, good masters vs. evil ones. I wish it was as clear as in the movies, books or fables. Alas, in real life it is very much a grey area, a place of shady characters concealing their intentions and true selves. The motivation behind a Sensei is not always gallant, where there is money to be made and power to be gained, there will always be bad people trying to abuse situations to their benefit. I think it is important to highlight both sides.

In most of my books I show the light and positive side of Karate. In this one I'll focus on the dark and dirty reality of Karate. I'll do my best to present it in a light and humorous way, and I hope that this will be useful to others. Helping you to see through the smoke and mirrors and navigate through stormy waters when joining a club or organisation. This story is based on my personal experience over 25 years of training in Karate and wrestling. Having seen high ranking meetings, political wars and personal games. I have changed all of the names used in this work; any coincidental events are not intentional.

I have to say that this project was on my mind for a few days before the 1st of April. As a prank I developed a cover for the book - just for fun. To my surprise I got quite a few massages with questions about where the book can be purchased. After explaining that this was a joke, I was encouraged to actually write it! So hey, in response to the demand, here we are in the dark corner of our little hell called Karate. I think most experienced martial artists will be able to relate to one or more of the stories in this book. Let's dive into the shitstorm and try to find our way! Hoist the sails and let's start our cruise...

Chapter 1 - The Old Master

He opened his eyes, looked about and saw three of his best students around his bed. He knew that his time was up, those three men were his best students. He also realised that a shitstorm is coming and it is going to hit soon. It will hit hard with anger and greed, fuelled by hunger. Hunger for power, money and influence. Worst of all is that he was powerless to do anything about it now. All his life the old master was trying to install rightfulness in his pupils, he failed. Now too frail to do anything he is hoping that one of those students will be a good choice as a successor, but which one?

They all have been loyal to him and his vision, all had promoted his values. It seems that they are happy to work together, yet there is something disturbing in the aura of these men, a shadow lingering and the unease, the master can sense it. He is not aware of who is truly good and who is just an imposter. He decides to share his organisation equally and wishes that they work together for the benefit of mankind promoting his Karate, he closes his eyes and his spirit rises up. Leaving the empty shell of his body on the bed surrounded by his students. As a last look he hovers above those who are living and listens. What he is witnessing would boil his blood, but now there is not a single drop of it in him, he cannot express in any way his disappointment in those in whom he had put his trust. He feels sorry for one of his pupils, the one who wanted to fulfil his wish. He knows that his positive attitude is a weakness that will be used against him. The old master wishes that he had seen this when he was alive and could make amends but it's too late. Now the shitstorm is gaining momentum, sending waves through his Karate world.

This short story is how I imagine most Karate masters would feel, seeing their students' behaviour after their death. A sad view of egos ruining their vision. Most of the organisations (that I'm aware of) have had political storms soon after the passing of their leader. From family run organisations, traditional schools both Okinawan and Japanese to modern Karate groups. The fight for power, money, influence and students is on! Not that it started just after the event of death, oh no, it was running a long time before that behind the scenes, making sure that the master was unaware. Little moves in the game, climbing up the ladder, making connections, creating alliances, making traps for the competition. I have seen this so many times, maybe because from the very beginning I was thrown into the deep end of the poo pool? Or maybe because my teacher hated politics and always rebelled against it. He has paid the price of being marginalised and not getting the recognition that he deserved. He always said he was happy to pay the price for independence! Now after 25 years and a few organisations I can see the value in that and just like him I'm independent and willing to move on, at the first sign of political games.

Let me describe what is happening within a big organisation when the master is headed to the eternal dojo.

First everyone mourns the death of the master, as it

is a good way to show how respectful you are. A few weeks later the cracks start to appear, usually at the first meeting of the most advanced / powerful students. Then the hunger for ultimate power comes out, most of the "leaders" start their game to gain as many followers as they possibly can at all cost.

Disputes about the future direction of the organisation starts, as everyone has a different view on what the master wanted. One thing is uniting them - every single one of them thinks that they are the one! The one who has been shown the true way by the teacher. They are the chosen one to lead this organisation. A few examples of this include Bruce Lee (I know Kung fu not Karate) is one of the top examples, most of the organisations are actively fighting one another with claims of I was the best student / I was the most recent student / I was the closest student etc. Next on the list would be Mas Oyama. After his passing we have countless organisations claiming that their way is the one and only for Kyokushin. Shotokan is the same, so many organisations claiming that they are relaying the real teachings of Funakoshi. Recently Taika Oyata sadly passed away. There are so many resulting factions, all doing the only and best way that Taika taught.

If you look deep into the motivation behind these factions it has nothing to do with keeping the master's legacy alive, it is all about using the master's name to gain power and money. Usually those who really want to preserve the direction that master would have wanted for the organisation are eliminated as they are a threat to the grand plan.

Next is the start of the factions. Influential instructors try to get people to support them as a successor. All means necessary are allowed - lies, bad mouthing, bribing etc. Everything that works can be used just to get members behind a given master.

The next step is to split and start one's own organisation - the one and only true organisation, that the Old Master would have definitely approved of. Now it's all about gaining momentum, which is best started by giving grades, titles and influence to members that have bigger clubs in exchange for moving away from the current organisation.

After establishing their organisation, it needs to be promoted as the only and best one, actively fighting off the others. Changes in the curriculum must be introduced no matter how stupid, always supported by "tradition".

The last step needs to be implemented now: control of members so they don't get too powerful and try to dethrone the new master. If the new master is lucky one day he will open his eyes on his death bed and realise that now he is just like his old master. The cycle has completed and it will start again. This is the law of the Dark side of Karate...

Chapter 2 - Baptism of Fire

I like to call this dark side of Karate the shitstorm, my friend likes to call it little Karate hell. It really doesn't matter how you describe it, sooner or later, whether you like it or not all students will be involved to some degree in martial arts politics.

Within my first month of joining my first Karate club I received a baptism of fire. I didn't even know what was going on – I was completely oblivious to the war that was raging within the club. Out of the blue I was told that I needed to choose, am I going with Student A or staying with the Master? As I had not been in the club long and had spent most of my time training with Student A, and most of the other students were going with Student A, I decided to join them and become a part of a new emerging global organisation, which to my mind meant high quality.

Now let me fill you in on the back story that I have discovered many years later, a story told to me by the Old Master. Some 17 years later it transpires that this story was as equally inaccurate as that told by Student A. The truth lies somewhere in between, as usual.

Just prior to me being forced to choose sides, Student A was explaining to all the club members how unhappy he was with the decisions of the Old Master. The decisions revolved around not joining new organisations and their structures. Those structures were offering great opportunities to train with Asian masters (including the head of a global organisation). Joining would have also meant that our club would become a part of a big group in Polish Karate and would therefore have given access to competitions. Sounds great right? What he had hidden from us at this point was that the Old Master had just told him that he was not ready to be graded for black belt. After training for more than ten years he believed that he was ready and part of the organisation deal was that he would be instantly graded to black belt. Don't read that as he was automatically given the belt, he did have to undergo a test. Thanks to the teachings of the Old Master he passed as one of the best in that organisation. His tactics were to put the Old Master in a bad light. Telling us what a bad person he is, how much alcohol he drinks, that he doesn't care about his students and that he just wants money and therefore holds students back from grading and doesn't allow them to take part in competition. Being an anxious 17-year-old boy who wanted desperately be a part of something, the choice was simple. We were joining the new organisation.

Soon enough my best friend and I noticed that the promised organisation was far from perfect, the entrenched politics was so obvious. Factions within the organisation had been fighting each other and the technical level was poor. This was sort of to be expected when you think about it. If you get dropouts and belt chasers from other organisations creating a new one, what do you expect? We never saw the Asian master at any of the events, we just received letters from him and a picture from one of the western magazines. The competitions were disappointing with the judging panel being extremely biased. I was stripped of a medal on many occasions for imaginary rule infringements. For example, I fought for two rounds with someone from another country, a Kyokushin guy and an excellent fighter. At the end of our bout I won by decision. All five referees pointed to my win, and yet the main judge called all of the referees to the table and we were told to fight again. Now, let's take a pause here and I'd like you to guess what the reason for overturning the decision was… Let me tell you as I wouldn't expect you guess it in a million years. I was adjusting my hair too much during the fight! At the time I had long hair, so yes, I did have to adjust it now and then, but never during the round, only when the time was stopped. I think this response was an advantage for my opponent as my focus was off from fighting. I was so shocked that in the extra round I lost my focus completely and got knocked down, and my opponent won. Our team's protest was dismissed, my opponent's protest was dismissed – my opponent was a true gentleman and an honest chap. We are now good friends. After the fight all of the referees came over to me with apologies, explaining that for the expansion and benefit of the organisation I had to lose, so that it would encourage that nation to take part in future tournaments. That day I decided that this organisation is not for me, so did my best friend.

As my friend had been training for much longer than me, we decided to find the Old Master and ask him if we could train with him privately. As a result of the split, he was left without any students and so decided to stop teaching. We managed to convince him to teach us. He was never angry with me over my choice as I had no way of knowing. He was disappointed with my friend, but understood his desire to take part in competitions. He arranged for both of us to join a bigger organisation that was run by his friend. I didn't like training there, but my friend was enjoying it and he went on to become a multiple times world champion in that organisation. I, on the other hand, became the Old Masters uchi deshi (apprentice). I learned from the Old Master about Student A's motives and how bad he was, obsessed with having a black belt and driven by power. Many years later I learned that Student A was also right about some aspects in relation to the Old Master, and so I too parted ways from him. I was very disappointed in how I was treated despite my total commitment to the promotion, organisation and teaching of Shin Ai Do Karate.

I have to say though that my Old Master has taught me not to trust organisations, he has fine-tuned my senses to detect bullshit, and in a lot of big organisations you only need look at the clock in the dojo to realise that it's always 'bullshit o'clock'. You are the target standing on a red X being hunted by professional killers. Exactly the same as in a car dealership.

Chapter 3 - Games

As you now know how I ended up joining a new organisation in the hope of some fun training where we could test ourselves in tournaments and master our art, let's have a look at how these types of organisations work. Note that this does not apply to all organisations, just those that are toxic. If you are in a great and supportive organisation then I'm very happy for you, alas I was not so fortunate. These thoughts represent an amalgamation of my insights across three organisations, two that I was a part of, and one that I am aware of from reputable sources. I'm sure that there will be a few people reading this that can relate to these scenarios.

It usually starts with a student. A student that wants to be great. He believes from the very beginning that he is the worthy one, and that it is his duty to lead the organisation. The aforementioned student is average in Karate, but he is great at making friends and connections. He ascends the hierarchy of the organisation and becomes a Sensei, maybe even a Shihan. He visualises himself at the top. He uses his influence to gain supporters, executes cunning plans, and eliminates the competition. Then he hits a glass ceiling – either people figure out that he is not honest and no longer want him in the association, or he becomes a threat to the leader and needs to be stopped, moved, or placated so as to remain content with his current position. However, this Sensei is a good businessman and has big clubs with lots of members. The organisation is desperate to keep him, but the current leader wants to maintain power. A conflict is inevitable, resulting in either the removal of the Sensei or his resignation. Now the bargaining starts. All organisations want students so that they can make money, in order to survive and thrive they need members who will pay. Our Sensei has a few options in this situation:

1. Leave for a competing organisation where he can be higher in the hierarchy
2. Leave for a more prestigious organisation
3. Create his own organisation

Choosing the Competition for Influence

If he chooses to migrate to a competing organisation then he will start to negotiate how much he can get out of the deal. On the table will be grades, titles, fees, and functions within the organisation. There is a custom in this kind of transition that when you change from one organisation to another you automatically get promoted a grade or two as a goodwill gesture. Often with additional titles such as Shihan, Kyoshi etc. In some cases, the organisation will throw in a position like Technical Advisor or Head Judge – you get the idea.

The negotiation is for a slice of the organisation. "I have so many students, how much will they have to pay to the organisation, and what is my cut from that? You know how expensive it is to change logos, banners, badges etc. so what sort of deal can I get for doing all of this?"

Regional powers also come into play, just as in the past where feuding kingdoms and lords fought over power and influence. If our Sensei will get a larger region to overlook and gain control of more clubs, he will be happy for some time. Yet in his mind this is just another step closer to becoming the emperor of Karate.

More Prestige

With this option our Sensei is willing to be temporarily downgraded, as he knows that with the reputation of the mother organisation, he will be able to get more students and start the process all over again.

Most large organisations are looking for new clubs to join their ranks. If our Sensei has many clubs, he can negotiate a better deal for himself. I was a part of that kind of organisation. Our Sensei accepted the downgrade and had to spend some time in the Hombu (headquarters) dojo, to convince the leaders that he was worthy. With over 130 clubs in a country where the mother organisation did not have a branch, it's easy to guess what the result was. Being a country representative had boosted his status from that of an outsider to a top player, with the backing of the Kancho (head of the family (organisation)). However, he took a big risk as some of his member clubs ran away, as the Kancho ordered that everyone will have to re-grade to meet his standards. Some got scared at the thought of this and abandoned ship.

Creation

If you don't like your current organisation there is always the option of leaving and creating your own. There is nothing wrong with this when you have reached a certain level of proficiency in given martial arts. I'm a real believer in making Karate your own and being independent. However, I cannot endorse people who reach a grade of 7th kyu and then go off and start their own system, promoting themselves to 10th dan. I know of two organisations where this has happened, where individuals were not happy with their speed of progression, and driven by their delusions of grandeur they left their organisations and created their own. The sad thing is that both of these still operate today and thanks to their connections in the political world they are quite successful, and students are misled into believing that they are training in genuine Karate.

There will always be a combination of these three key behaviours being undertaken in the martial arts world, all having one goal, to achieve power. Power drives people to do bad things, as said by Lord Acton *"Absolute power corrupts absolutely"*. In search of total control, they will not stop at anything till they get what they want.

Chapter 4 - Master of Puppets

This example is from an organisation that I was a part of for a very brief period of time, but I have insight into it through good friends who went on to be either top athletes or great instructors for that organisation, until they learnt about the organisations problems and moved on. This is a sad story as the master became the puppet and the student the puppet operator.

It all started in the eighties when a big split started in one of the leading organisations. In search of prestige one dojo owner found a respectful master. The new master joined his dojo under his leadership and had huge success. With time his success grew and money was flooding his wallet, what more could he want? There was a problem though. The old master was getting old and our "hero" wanted to be a worthy successor. Unfortunately, this was not possible as there was someone else much closer to the old master. Someone who couldn't be removed, belittled, or made to quit, he was a part of the old master's bloodline.

There must be another way for our hero to achieve his goals? He is a strong character who rules his organisation with an iron fist. Rewarding loyal supporters and threatening and crushing any resistance. He is one of the first Karate practitioners in the country, the one who fought in top competitions, he is worth of being Soke! His plan is going to take years, but he is in no rush – he is also a great strategist. The plan is in place, in the beginning the old master was included in all meetings and had a voice. Over the years slowly, step by step, those ties were removed. With age the old master's health and wits had deteriorated, so it was easier to manipulate him. There was one more factor against the old master, he really liked the student and trusted him, why wouldn't he? This student had been a loyal follower for years, always nice, paying membership fees on time, inviting the old master regularly for seminars, examinations etc. His cooperation was flawless. The old master was not aware of the game being played behind the scenes and the true character of his pupil. As is often the case, manipulative characters are very capable liars, and highly likeable too. They can deceive, cheat, like and pretend for as long as they are not caught or until they have achieved their goal.

As I was saying, this is a sad story as with the aging old master our hero started to push his boundaries. Eventually bloodline contenders started to notice what was going on and began to prepare amendments to the contract on how things will be run in the future. The time came when the old master decided that it would be best for the organisation for him to retire and a new leader appointed. Our hero was furious, the power was slipping out of his hands, his prestige was threatened, he was not in a position to start over with a new association, maybe being downgraded or staying with this organisation under a new leader would cut off his power and benefits. There must be a way! And so, he found a way to use the old master for one last time. Let's organise a goodbye seminar to pay our respects to the old master. In that last seminar the old master was convinced (I have no idea how) that he should create a new organisation with our hero as a leader and the old master as a patron, to allow the use of his name. All of the papers were ready, they just needed a signature. I can imagine that this was the most difficult part, but our hero managed to pull it off. Within a few days it all went through the courts and was registered. Now even if the old master objects nothing can be done. The organisation is registered with our hero at the top. His dream had come true, he is the head of the international organisation. There was a minor hiccup as members of the organisation soon got information about what had happened from the appointed leader and decided to leave. Then our hero started to harvest clubs and individuals to rebuild members and payments, collecting all types of individuals that were unwanted in other organisations. I have to say that it must be working as now, so many years later, they are still going strong.

Unfortunately, this is not something that is rare. It has happened for ages. Let me use again the lords and emperors analogy – games, cunning plans, treason and murder are parts of the power gain strategy. Luckily for us, in this day and age people do not kill others so frequently, and so everything revolves around games. Sadly, the old master passed away a few months after retiring. He was a great fighter and coach; I have a lot of respect for him.

Chapter 5 - Fear of the...

In this chapter let's investigate a story about, let's call him Sensei B, who joined as a young student the dojo of Master C. This is a story about protecting power and influence. It can happen in any organisation where the leader wants to retain the top position and feels threatened by another instructor. An instructor who does not necessarily have ill intentions, but is just simply a great teacher, businessman / businesswoman or is charismatic.

Sensei B joined the club of Master C because he wanted to get strong and hoped to become a great fighter. He put all of his heart into training and has been a dedicated follower and propagator of the strongest Karate. Through his commitment to training he quickly began to stand out in the dojo and soon in the whole of the organisation. Master C was very pleased. The young student was a promising fighter and he was also liked by others, at that point. Sensei B wanted to be the best at what he was doing. The countless hours of training paid off and he soon became the best fighter in the dojo and was promoted to black belt. Shortly after this achievement, Sensei B showed promising teaching skills and was a good candidate for becoming an instructor. The decision by Master C to make Sensei B and instructor turned out to be a great one and Sensei B soon had a dedicated group of students at the dojo. As he was a trusted student and his loyalty was never in question, he was chosen to promote Master C's Karate at another location. Sensei B was allowed to open his own dojo and become a branch chief. He opened his modest dojo and focussed on promoting Master C's teachings. Soon enough his dojo grew, and the best fighters in the organisation started to attend Sensei B's classes.

With the success of his first dojo, he was given permission to expand and open a new location. The story repeated itself and in a short time, Sensei B had a string of successful dojos where many of the top fighters wanted to train. Master C was very happy - the new branch was generating more and more money and his style was becoming famous. Sensei B was completely dedicated to Master C and fully focussed on growing and proving the strength of his master's Karate. He had a recipe for success and continued to work hard.

Over a short period of time Sensei B's branch grew into a multi-dojo, mini organisation. Sensei B started to develop his methods of teaching, creating his own style within the Style. As the students who studied Sensei B's methods began to dominate tournaments and the expansion of his training groups continued, it was only a matter of time before other senseis within the organisation became disgruntled. Some of the other branch chiefs were jealous of Sensei B's success and engaged in political games to restrict his expansion. Their power, influence and income were under attack. Students were moving from their dojos to Sensei B's. Something had to be done!

The senseis decided the best approach was to inform Master C about a threat to his leadership, and they began spreading rumours about plans for dethroning the Master and taking over his Karate empire. At that moment, Master C started to realise that the rumours could become a reality, and doubt started to creep in. What should he do about the young, super successful Sensei B? His first action was to order a stop to the expansion, which loyal Sensei B accepted without complaint; he even offered to withdraw his presence so as to not intimidate other senseis. This was not enough to pacify those that had complained, as their students would still travel to Sensei B's brand new, big dojo. This sensei needs to be eliminated. So, more games, rumours, and complaints ensued.

Under pressure from so many and in fear of losing supporters, Master C had to act. Despite his admiration of his student, he ordered him to move to another country in order to promote his Karate. Sensei B declined the offer, not wanting to abandon his students and not wanting his work to be destroyed. His decision infuriated the other instructors, and the pressure grew on Master C. Sensei B must be stopped or many other dojos will leave the organisation. Master C's options were limited. The choice wasn't an easy one, but one had to be made, Sensei B had to be removed. And so, it was done. A good member of the organisation whose devotion and loyalty were unquestionable was now expelled, with a broken heart.

Sensei B was left without a choice. He had many students and so the only reasonable course of action was to start his own organisation, becoming a direct competitor to Master C. What Master C didn't foresee was that a great number of students would follow Sensei B, resulting in a great chunk of his organisation leaving. The mediocre senseis that had played the game had much less of a following. In hindsight it would have been better to remove them and keep Sensei B.

Leaders of big organisations often forget how it is to be a student, and how students will behave. For most students the brand of Karate and the logo on their gi is irrelevant. More important is who their teacher is, and 90% of students will follow their teacher and be happy to wear a new logo. The removal of a potential threat also showed other talented instructors in the organisation what awaited them if they dared to become too successful. Since Sensei B's departure, a great number of instructors left Master C in order to create their own organisations.

Chapter 6 - Bribery

Our hero is now the leader of his own organisation, let's call it the Super Karate Association of Masters, or SKAM for short. Establishing his own organisation feels great and his feeling of self-worth has shot through the roof, and yet he doesn't understand why other instructors aren't flocking to his organisation? How can this be? The Great Supreme Leader, Kancho, Hanshi, Shihan with the Menkyo Kaiden certificate is obviously not getting the recognition he deserves! This situation is unjust and needs to be amended, maybe one more dan will help to get people onboard? Or maybe he has gone a step too far? He has already given himself the rank of 10th dan in SKAM, but there are others who hold 11th, maybe that's the problem? Regardless of his decision on his next dan, he needs to get more people through the door. So, he will get to work on marketing.

He begins his campaign of promoting his new organisation as superior to others, in order to fish for those who are not happy with their current organisation, those seeking fame or another grade or two. There will be the official slogans:

- "Come to us and you will see what real quality is."
- "We have the best competitions."
- "Our instructor programme is the best."

There will also be methods of persuasion that entice instructors to join SKAM via back channels:

- Belts given away
- Financial incentives
- Influence and power

I share with you here two stories about bribery. The first is about stealing students, and the second is about getting instructors to join a new organisation. In the first instance I was a witness and acted on what I had seen to make my friends aware of what was happening. The second story was directly targeted at me – an offer was made to me behind my teacher's back while he was still in an arena with me. Both cases were unfortunately conducted by representatives from highly reputable organisations and I'm guessing that these offers were made by individuals who wanted to grow their clubs.

Snatching Students

The arena was full, spectators were talking loudly and showing support for the fighters. I met with my friend from another part of this foreign country. It was a treat to be watching those fighters in this top tournament. Sensei D and I were sitting in the middle row, behind us sat my student and a couple of Sensei D's students. We had a chat about how our dojos were performing and generally catching up. Then we met Sensei E. Sensei D knew him. I had heard about him. We chatted for a bit and Sensei E explained that he had just changed his organisation, but within the same style, and that his students were taking part in this tournament. We now had someone to cheer for and support. The fighting went on and there were some spectacular bouts. My mind was itching with my memories of taking part in these events and my 20-year-old brain was whispering, "You can do it, let's get competing!". Suddenly I was dragged away from my daydreaming by a conversation – "Here's my business card boys if you want to join my dojo and get some real Karate training." I looked at Sensei D, he looked back at me and smiled. I whispered "Can you hear that?". Sensei D said "Of course I can." "Will you do anything about it?" I asked. "No." he replied. "It is up to my students to choose where they want to train. I teach the way I teach and if they are not happy then maybe they should move." I felt that this was a great approach. Sensei D had no signs of insecurity, he was sure that his students would stay with him, in the same way that I was sure about my student.

Sensei E chatted to us a bit more and then went away to see his fighters. Smiling and complementing us on our work and Karate. For me it was the fakest smile ever. After he left our students tapped us on the shoulders and showed us his business card, expressing their feelings, which can be summarised in three words – what a dick!

Unfortunately snatching students is the norm, not just within Karate organisations, but everywhere. Offering financial incentives, belts, and opportunities is a daily business. Some students fall for it, others stick to their guns. As coaches, we can only do the best that we can and let our students choose what they want. It is painful when students are leaving, but they have to follow their own path. From my experience I know that it's not often a pleasant experience for them, as the new organisation is just using them for their own gains.

Cajoling Coaches

I was always a part of an independent club and had never really truly belonged to any big organisation. We were affiliated to a larger association, but on independent terms, and I still continue with this approach to this day.

Many offers were made to try to get my teacher to assimilate into organisations, which he always declined. Another offer had just been made at this tournament, the Polish Cup of one of the smaller organisations. However, the offer was not from them, but from an emerging organisation that had just started in Poland. The Polish branch chief knew my teacher from the 'old days' when he was a teenager and my teacher was higher in the ranks of Kyokushin. Sensei F came to Sensei G and said that he had just become the branch chief of this new organisation that was coming to Poland, which will take over all of the contact Karate in Poland, with him at the top. Sensei F said that he would really like Sensei G to join him and be a technical advisor to the new organisation. Sensei G just looked at him and burst into laughter, and then said "No.". Sensei F left deflated, and I thought that was the end of it. When Sensei G went to support one of our fighters on the tatami, Sensei F appeared next to me. He introduced himself as the top person within this new organisation, and proceeded to paint a bright future for me, if I left Sensei G. "You will have access to the best teachers in the world, tournaments all over the planet, and I can give you a black belt when you join." I was a brown belt at the time so he thought I would be tempted by the bait of becoming a black belt without an examination, which says a lot about him. I declined, explaining that I liked it where I was. In a last-ditch effort, he offered me a second dan to come onboard. I was gobsmacked! At the time I thought, naively, that Karate was full of honourable people and that you can't just get or buy grades. How wrong I was...

I spoke with Sensei G about what had happened. Sensei G explained that Sensei F was always average at best in Karate, but he always wanted to be great and therefore went to great lengths to get grades without putting the work in. He had achieved 4th dan at the time by jumping from one organisation to another, with a questionable reputation, but had somehow managed to blag a reputable one.

I wonder how many of this sort of dan grade are out there? People who will do anything in the pursuit of promotion, and how many organisations take those people on in order to sustain their income / image.

Coming back to our hero and his SKAM organisation. He is now travelling around, visiting clubs, tournaments, and seminars. Promoting, selling, and bribing people to join his little empire. Soon enough SKAM will grow, with all of those who were looking for something better, or those who just wanted to climb higher in the hierarchy of martial arts. The sad part about all of this is that there will be people like myself who just want to train who get caught in the crossfire. Those who will find themselves in this dysfunctional environment and who are totally unaware of all of the shit that is going on. There will also be a fair amount of people who are in even deeper shit and are just trying to get out of it – joining the promising new organisation as a means of escape!

As you probably know, no scammer will honestly advertise their scam. It would be very refreshing to see a Karate organisation putting out a slogan like this: "Join our organisation, we are easy going, we give out belts, we want your money, nothing else. Join in and I will feel more powerful. Best wishes, Kaicho Biggus Dickus."

I continue to stay away from big organisations, and I recommend that you do in depth research before you decide to join or change your association. If you have been offered any incentives that seem questionable, my advice – stay away!

Chapter 7 - Good Times

I've mentioned in previous chapters that my teacher never joined a big organisation, however, we did join a smaller association. He had a dislike of massive, homogeneous corporations, as is often found in Karate organisations, but he was keen on multi-style, democratic structures. So, we became a part of association "I". It was great and everything about it was brilliant. Nice people, nice events, respect for everyone all round. In particular, I really admired the chairman, who I've become good friends with. He ran the association in a very open way, always with others in mind. For years the cooperation ran flawlessly, and yet none of us noticed the darkness lurking within.

As is usually the case in these stories, evil emerges after times of prosperity. This case was no different. One of the instructors was growing in influence and power, silently, behind the scenes, let's call him Shihan H. I thought I was good friends with this person and I had the utmost respect for him. He was collaborating with another sensei (let's call him Sensei I) who I knew was a bit, how should I put it - suspicious. I didn't like him, and formally he was not a part of this association. He had his own group and attended as a guest at our seminars. I later learned of some issues surrounding him and how our story will wind up intertwined in a shitstorm, but you'll have to wait a bit for that story, which is covered in Chapter 9 - Demolition Man.

Anyway, coming back to the good times... My Karate training had matured so much during this time as I had trained with so many excellent instructors in Association I. I learned how to use Karate as a form of meditation, I had participated in many philosophical conversations with top instructors and this had expanded my horizons significantly. I met people from all over the world, trained with them in multiple systems and became used to being taken out of my comfort zone. I got involved in many projects and became friends with people who have since become mentors for me in areas that I am lacking. Most of the instructors within this group were completely oblivious to what was happening in the background, including myself. If you had asked me at the time if I would have suspected that Shihan H would become a tyrant I would have laughed, he was one of the nicest people I had ever met.

The rule in this association was that the chairman was elected every four years, and once elected, that person could not be re-elected for some time. Sounds like a fair system, right? Indeed, if you have the right people at the top. During my time in this association, I was a member under three different chairmen. Two of them were amazing in that role and I thank them for the great experience. What then proceeded to happen was just like in the Stanford Prison Experiment (SPE) that was conducted in the 1970s by Philip Zimbardo, where regular people turned into sadistic tyrants. If the conditions are right, giving people power over others without consequences turns most people into cruel beasts. Not that I'm insinuating that the aforementioned Shihan turned into a beast, I'm sure that he's still a nice person, but in the realms of this association he morphed into a bully. His work behind the scenes had paid off; not only was he elected as the chairman, but was also named as the successor of his system. He had suddenly changed from being a nice, quiet chap into a demanding boss.

At the beginning there were immediate, small changes, which seemed to be reasonable. We all have our own vision of what evolution looks like and so I went along with these changes, as did the others. The changes didn't have much of an impact on me as by that time I was living in the UK and my task was to make connections and build a structure for the association over here.

Everything changed when it was my turn to organise an international seminar in order to promote the association. What would you do to organise such an event in a new country? Perhaps you'd invite people who you know might potentially be interested in joining, right? So, I invited a few instructors that I had become friends with. Some of them had been a great help when I had just arrived in the UK, and so I wanted them to meet this awesome association and the people that made it great. Then the shitstorm clouds started to form, and the first lightning bolt struck via an email. (Please note that I'm paraphrasing the content of the email exchange below.)

Dear Les,

I hope you are well. I look forward to joining you at your event. We are very happy that you are a part of our organisation. You do amazing work to promote our values. However, please be advised that these individuals are not able to take part in your seminar.

> *Sensei 1*
> *Sensei 2*
> *Sensei 3*

Please remove them immediately.

Best wishes,

Tyrant no1, aka the boss.

I was so puzzled that I thought it was a joke, so naturally I replied:

Dear Boss aka Tyrant no1,

Thank you for your email. I do not understand your message, I was given a task to promote our organisation in this foreign land. I'm organising this event and I think these individuals are a valuable asset to our future structures in the UK. They also personally helped me in building my dojo here. So please explain why they should not take part in the seminar.

Kind regards,

Les.

And in that instant the shitstorm broke with a furore that I did not anticipate…

Chapter 8 - Ubiquitous Shitstorm

Karateka often think that our art is special, the chosen one perhaps. The reality is that it isn't, what is happening in Karate is happening everywhere else. Political games are present in every activity where there is something to be made (power, money etc.). From experience I know that Karate is a big fish in a small pond. As a part of my wrestling training, I had the opportunity to attend a few meetings on Olympic wrestling in both an official and a social capacity. The latter involving alcohol. The Latin phrase *"in vino veritas"* meaning that under the influence of alcohol someone tells the truth is spot on! This philosophy was tested many times in Poland under communism, where you did not know who to trust and so most deals were agreed over a few bottles of vodka. Unfortunately, this has led to many people in Poland becoming alcoholics.

Going back to wrestling. Because both Greco-Romano and Freestyle wrestling styles are included in the Olympics, there are huge sums of money involved. Government grants, funding, and sponsorship are all at stake, easily running into millions of pounds. Every country wants to produce the top athletes, right? National governing bodies have access to bespoke sports facilities that cost millions to build and run. If you are in a top position then you have all of that money at your disposal. You get to decide who gets funding, equipment and coaches. It is a fearful competition and the game is on at all times. Every move of every coach is tracked by others. There are floating coalitions that wax and wane depending on the current needs and possible benefits.

At one of the meetings that I attended most of the coaches got drunk. I don't actually drink that much and so I was pretending to keep up with everyone else. As I was sober, I had the chance to listen to (and remember!) the conversations taking place around me. This meeting was during a competition that lasted for three days, so it was fairly safe as no one was driving anywhere. The amount of backstabbing and fakery going on in that room would put Game of Thrones to shame. In every corner there were ongoing debates and commentary on which would be the best ways to take control of money or how to gain more money for their clubs. Promises were made on how the money would be shared after each power takeover; endless possibilities were dreamt up. Fights and disputes were cropping up all over the place as alcohol induced animosities surfaced and no one could control their temper. For me it was a shocking experience to see top coaches and elite athletes, including Olympic medallists, behaving in that way. If Karate really wants to be a political shitshow, it has a lot to learn.

I also witnessed their political games on a much smaller scale in a coalition of a few clubs, where an official union was created with an elected president, vice-president, secretary and so on. I was just a regular member. Even just being an also-ran in this coalition didn't shield me from people trying to get my support with promises of me escalating the power ladder. These types of games always end with a grand finale, when a volcano of shit mixed with emotions explodes and showers everyone. Usually this marks the end of the coalition, with members disembarking the organisation and reshuffling to start again under a new name, and the cycle starts again. The shitshow must go on. There will always be someone who thinks that he or she deserves better and where money and power are involved, all moves are allowed.

Chapter 9 - Demolition Man

I sent an email to Tyrant no1 and was pissed off about the whole situation, but my wife convinced me not to act hastily (which I'm renown for doing and often regret later). Her view was that something had been lost in translation, and that I should wait for an answer before jumping to any conclusions. So, I listened to her and impatiently waited for a response. Soon enough an email arrived, and straight away I was pissed off even more!

Dear Les,

I'm the head of the association and I say what is going to happen.

> *Sensei 1*
> *Sensei 2*
> *Sensei 3*

Will not take part in the seminar, as I don't wish them to be at this event.

I was fuming, I had steam coming out of my ears and my blood was boiling. Just to add insult to injury, at the end of the email was a threat:

If you do not comply, I will suspend your status as a representative for the UK.

Best wishes,

Soke Tyrant no1.

In the meantime, I contacted my friend (Sensei 1) to ask why he might not be wanted at the seminar. Guess what, it turned out that Sensei I (the one that I had an aversion to) and Sensei 1 knew each other, and they did not get on. And so, Sensei I made a request that Sensei 1 be excluded. I wrote back to Tyrant no1.

Hi Tyrant no1,

I understand that you have been selected to be the head of the association, but I'm an independent member and no one will tell me who I can and can't invite to my seminar.

The whole concept of our association is to promote friendship, and your leadership is opposing this philosophy, which I strongly disagree with.

I also don't understand why Sensei I is getting involved in the internal matters of our association?

As I will not tolerate threats, I'm tending my formal resignation as a representative in the UK and resigning as an association member.

Best wishes,

Les.

This is what I wrote - in my heart I wanted to write something else, but once again my lovely wife stopped me from doing it my way.

Little did I know that my decision would instigate a domino effect. I sent an email to my friends explaining the reasons for my resignation and expected to continue alone as a result. However, to my surprise my teacher supported my decision and left with me. A few days later I received an email that another Polish branch had also withdrawn from the association. A week later I got a call from an ex-president of the association asking me what had actually happened, and so I explained. He tried his best to mediate and remedy this situation but faced huge resistance. A few weeks later he discovered that Tyrant no1 was spreading untrue information about me and had placed me on the wall of shame for traitors. Spreading lies is very common for people with insecurities as they try to build their persona as someone that is rightful and a victim in these circumstances. After several weeks of negotiations, the ex-president told me that he too was quitting and that he cannot believe how Tyrant no1 has changed and cannot be reasoned with. He had become obsessed about his power and would not have anyone telling him what to do.

After the ex-president had left a few other countries and dojo's left the association in disbelief. As a consequence of my resignation the association had gone from being a multination organisation promoting friendship and cooperation to a small collective of a few dojos that were closed and focussed on glorifying Tyrant no1.

A few years after this event even more dojos left,

leaving the association a shadow of its former self.

Although I'm sad that the association was broken up, I'm relieved that so many people supported me and saw through the lies and games of Tyrant no1. I'm also glad that others appreciated my integrity and willingness to stand up to bullying. Personally, I'm not bothered if I'm a part of an association or not, so long as I can do what I think is right then I'm happy.

Since the breakup, all of the former members of that association have come together in a new organisation, and we see each other regularly at events.

Chapter 10 - Search for Independence

Having observed my teacher and his approach towards big organisations and having had my own limited experience at the time, I was predisposed to searching for independence.

If I said that I never wanted to be in a renowned organisation, that would be a lie. I have thought about it often, I had even argued with my teacher about the reasons why we should join a larger organisation. I guess my personal insecurities were projected onto my practice of Karate, I wanted gratification and confirmation that I do legitimate Karate. Recognition of our system supported by known lineage was something that I had romanticised about. In my mind it would automatically improve my Karate skills. Yet the more I spoke with my friends about their experiences of well-known organisations, the more I disliked the idea.

You might have picked up from previous chapters that I'm not a fan of being told what to do and how to do it, so as much as I wanted to be a part of a large organisation, I just wasn't prepared to give up my freedom by subscribing to one and only one Karate organisation. In my opinion a huge problem with the well-known organisations is that they seem to promote themselves as the only rightful style of Karate and brainwash their members into believing this. Or perhaps it is similar to religion – we as a species need to believe in something greater than ourselves, to give meaning to our lives, and we are willing to die for it. I've not felt that I needed this, I've never been religious nor obsessed about a particular style of Karate. In terms of my art, I'm a free spirit and a thief. If I see something that works and I like it, I steal it, and incorporate it into my Karate. This is an unthinkable practice in many of those organisations that are the protectors of the traditional, only true way of Karate.

Over my years of training, I have seen many things happen within our dojo, in other dojos and in organisations. I have generally stayed away in search of independence, even when I was a part of an organisation, I have stayed true to my beliefs and followed my internal compass. In the process I have managed to annoy many, acquire enemies and faced numerous shitstorms, but despite all of this I can look in the mirror and see a true self who never gives in. Years of sailing through a poo pond have paid off, and eventually I have found two organisations that I'm proud to be an independent member of. In these organisations I have all of the support that I need without any political agendas imposed on me. They are run by people who have martial arts and martial artists in mind instead of personal gains. I hope that they will continue to operate this way in the future. If they do change then there will be no hesitation on my part to walk away. To quote Riddick, *"I bow to no man."* (Or organisation!).

I'm all for cooperation and growth – together we are better, but it has to be with respect and freedom. I will make an exception in this chapter and name the two organisations, just in case you find yourself in a dire situation within your current organisation or you're an independent looking for support. I have found Isshindo Kan Europe to be a fantastic home for myself with real friends. It is a very small organisation where everyone knows each other personally. The sole purpose of this group is to promote the great values of martial arts. The second organisation is the British Combat Karate Association (BCKA) / World Combat Association, which is an umbrella organisation in the UK providing insurance, qualifications, gradings, and whatever you need to run a club. I highly value the BCKA as it has never interfered in the internal affairs of my dojo and yet it has always been keen to help with promotion, problem solving, or just answering my stupid questions. So, if you're searching for non-political organisations that treat their members fairly, I can highly recommend these two.

Chapter 11 - Your Way or the Highway

In martial arts, and life in general, having principles and values are key to development and real progression. If you stick to your values, you will always be able to look in the mirror and be proud. Don't take shortcuts, stay true to yourself. The journey might be bumpy and uncomfortable but it will be worth it. Below are a few rules that guide my approach to existing within a martial arts environment.

Have Courage

Most people associate courage with great events, like fighting a monster, slaying a dragon or going to war. What I see as courage is the ability to do what you know to be right when no one else is looking, or when you're in a situation where everyone else is doing something wrong. Karate is meant to be full of gallant knights in shiny pyjamas, pyjamas as pure and as white as their hearts. The reality is somewhat far from this idealistic view. Have the courage to stand up for your ideals or at least the courage to not partake in things that you don't approve of.

Be Committed

Commitment is simply when you don't feel like doing something that you persist and follow your actions through. If you have decided what your moral values are, you stick to them. It may be tough as others do not always hold the same values. You might be put under pressure to bend your principles but commit to your principles and be the person that you want to be.

Work Hard

Despite what others might offer, don't take shortcuts. Work hard to achieve your goals whilst still upholding your values. This not only applies to training, but also work hard on speaking out if something is unjust. It is easy to take a back seat and let others sort things out. If you can make a difference, work hard to make that difference.

Be Honest

Honesty, it's not just about being true to others. Not that you should lie to others, but you should undertake an honest assessment of yourself to find out who you are and what you want. What do you stand for? What does your organisation / teacher stand for? Review your values if they are not in line with those of your organisation – perhaps it is time to move on or to try and make a change within that organisation.

Use Your Initiative

Initiative is doing what needs to be done without being asked to do it. If you see that there are actions done by others within the organisation or by the organisation itself that are wrong, do something about it. Bring it up for discussion, offer your point of view and potential solutions. Ask questions, especially those that are difficult. If you don't do it no one else will (hopefully they might, but you never know).

Be Kind

This really shouldn't need explanation but I think a few words are important. We all should be kind to others, by kind I don't mean being a pushover, but be considerate of others and their perspectives. I can be kind but still stand firmly for my values.

Provide Leadership

If you run a club or a group, chances are you're a leader. Now the question is, what kind of leader are you? Are you one who uplifts people, or one who imposes your way on others? Be an inspiring leader where people clearly know what you stand for. Be transparent, it's not ideal if you preach about something in class and then do the opposite outside of the training hall – it's hard to be inspired by a hypocrite.

A leader is someone who takes the time to help

those in need. A leader doesn't stomp on people who need their help. A leader reaches down, grabs their hand and pulls them up.

Think Positively

Positive thinking is always a good habit to have, but I don't mean it in terms of having a happy outlook on life. We all go up and down on the spectrum of mental wellbeing. When we are happy, we go up, but when we are having a bad day, it drops back down. This is a normal part of life. What I'm talking about is having a positive outcome in mind. If I do something, my intention is to make a positive impact. Whether that be through teaching, working, or writing books like this one, in my mind I hope that I will have a positive impact. In this case I hope that this book will help you to avoid some of the political traps in martial arts.

Have Respect

In my mind there are two types of respect. The first is general respect, something that you show to everyone before you get to know them. You respect their rights as a person, this comes automatically. The second type is earned respect. This is developed as a result of a person's actions or their expertise in a given field.

In the context of the martial arts world, I think that it is important that you keep your first type of respect consistent. You might not respect a person for their behaviour or actions but keep your composure and treat them with respect. This will help you maintain your own values and not get dragged into petty squabbling. To quote George Bernard Shaw, *"I learned long ago, never to wrestle with a pig. You get dirty, and besides, the pig likes it."*

Be Tolerant

As we all know, everyone has a tolerance limit. It is up to you to honestly assess how much you can tolerate before having to take action. Something that boils my blood might be something that you do not find a problem at all. When you start training, try to establish your tolerance limits in terms of what is acceptable within your moral code, and assess this on a regular basis.

Be Resilient

Develop a thick skin, as in the world of greed and power no one will hold back. You will be on the receiving end of whatever they can throw at you in order to try and make you bend to their will. I have spoken with so many martial artists that are afraid of the consequences of them standing up to something or wanting to move on. They have been threatened by their 'so-called' leaders that their lives will be ruined, they will be subjected to physical violence etc. From experience I know how frustrating this is, but in most cases the reality is that nothing will happen at all. You just move on, find a new organisation and live happily. It might be that people from your past organisation criticise or say bad things about you, but if anything more serious happens then you always have the police and courts there to seek justice.

These are the rules that I follow. I hope that they are broadly similar to your personal moral compass and that we can stand together to make Karate a better place.

Chapter 12 - Everybody Lies

By saying that Karate is nothing special I might upset a few people. I mean no disrespect, I love the art of the empty / Chinese hands, I really do. That's why I've been doing it for over 25 years (at the time of writing) and I think it has many positive aspects to offer. What I mean by 'nothing special' is in relation to large organisations, soulless corporations like institutions that will do anything to extract money as fast as they can. This is the reality in which we live.

You can see the traits of money-making schemes all over the place. Car industries lie about emissions just to get more sales and increase their profits with disregard to human life, thanks Volkswagen. Fishing industries compete against each other with devastating effects on our environment and disregard for sustainability. Sports where most organisations fight each other with clubs scrabbling over power and influence.

Wherever you look something dodgy is going on, corruption is visible in every walk of life. I come from a country where corruption was normal. If you went to see a doctor the expectation was that an envelope with money would be passed to them, so as to ensure you got a better diagnosis or that the treatment received was not second class. It seems to me that this is human nature, to exploit others for our own gain. It is a huge challenge to not fall for that, especially if you run a club or have power over others in some way. There are a vast number of organisations and clubs out there, and there will always be a number of them that are rotten, hopefully there are more good ones than bad. We just need to realise that it's not peculiar to Karate. I would argue that Karate is a big fish in a small pond, but perhaps more to the point, it is our pond and we should do our best to take care of it so all of the little fish are safe.

Chapter 13 - Allies

If you decided to take the independent route for your Karate it might be a difficult path, the big corporations are against you. Their followers can be similar to those of a cult or religious fanatics; trying to destroy, discredit and break you on your journey. The most commonly used tools in these attacks are lineage and style. If you have neither of these, you are not credible. Even worse if you had these, but then decided to change some of the techniques or methodologies. In this case you are no longer a 'traditional' Karate-Ka and you should therefore be looking to join someone who has proper credentials. The problem is that 'traditional' is a very modern term to distinguish modified versions of Karate, but the blind followers fail to grasp this concept. If we look at what the masters of the past said about changing Karate, they all supported it and indeed, did it themselves! Itosu, Funakoshi, and Motobu all changed their Karate to suit their needs. This is what Funakoshi and others said about changes in martial arts:

> *"Times change, the world changes, and obviously the martial arts must change too."* - Funakoshi, Karate-Do My Way of Life

> *"Karate changes every few years. This change happens because a teacher will continue to learn and add his personality to the teachings."* - Choshin Chibana

"A kata is not fixed or immoveable. Like water, it's ever changing and fits itself to the shape of the vessel containing it." - Kenwa Mabuni

Based on these quotes I would suggest that change is not something to worry about, in fact it should be embraced. If your Karate is good then it's good. Just don't lie to yourself if it isn't. In the latter case having no lineage will not help and clubs like this will often prefer to join a corporate style of Karate organisation to gain credibility and hide behind fees and memberships.

I digress slightly. We are living in fortunate times where there are many independent dojos and organisations. Find the one that works for you, be sure to check them out and don't rush to join. Examine what the given organisation is doing, but don't just look at their overt actions, read between the lines and pay attention to what is not being said. In this way you learn much more. Speak to people. People like to talk, especially those who are not happy, they are likely to give you a broader view of the organisation.

Try aligning yourself with their approach to training. Is it working for you? Do you have the same values? There is no point in joining a Combat Group if you are interested in sport aspects and competition. You won't get the maximum benefit from that venture.

If you can find them, try reaching out to individuals

who have already gone through the same steps that you are planning to tread. There are many people out there who can help and advise you on what to do and what to avoid. Many of them will be happy and willing to help you to avoid the mistakes that they made along the way. Mentoring in this way is one of the key rules to success in martial arts. I will shamelessly plug my free book at this point, the "Rules for Success in Karate". In this book you can read in detail about what it takes to be successful in Karate. Details of where to find it are at the end of this book.

I regret waiting so long before reaching out to others when I arrived in the UK, it would have saved me a lot of hassle. I was fortunate to escape without harm, but I still managed to make the mistake of turning to an organisation for insurance where it transpired that the leader (who was of advanced years) had lost control of it and it turned out that I had been running my dojo for three years without insurance even though I had all of the paperwork. This organisation has gone now and the leader has passed away so I will not name and shame here, but the moral of the story is to thoroughly check who you are dealing with and to make sure that all of the i's are dotted and the t's crossed.

Getting as many allies as you can to support your group is very important, not only for your martial art, but also for your mental health as some organisations can be vicious – do your homework.

Summary

We have now journeyed through the different shades of darkness in Karate. I have deliberately focussed on organisations because we, as members, can influence and take action against what is happening around us. Without members even the best organisation is nothing, so the responsibility lies with us to keep things in check.

Like many others, I was led to believe that Karate improves a person's character, making them better, but now I have adjusted my view having seen how many martial artists are far from honest, nice, and loving people. Unfortunately, the very nature of martial arts organisations, with their grading structures, make them ideal places for predators to operate. Hierarchy alongside a culture of not asking questions and just doing what you're told can attract abusers and bullies. They may hide for years until they get to a position where they can start their abuse and unfortunately not enough is being done to highlight these situations. Karate always wants to protect its image and sweep bad things under the carpet, or deal with it behind the curtain of decency and building character. This is unfortunately a common behaviour that has been exhibited in other institutions from football to the church. We are all encouraged to not see or talk about bad things for the greater good. This greater good is obviously not the wellbeing of an organisation's members. Who would want to join an organisation where the main goal would be reaping money from people at the expense of covering up abuse? These organisations need to put out a grander ethos message that people can subscribe to. "Don't disrespect the master, it is your responsibility to carry the torch of a master who passed 100 years ago." Making people responsible for something greater than themselves and giving them the power to do this can make them do strange things in order to protect the leader of an organisation.

We must realise that most organisations are companies and therefore their main goal is to make money. The rest of their aspirations revolve around this and you or I are just a means of achieving that goal. If we are lucky the owner will run the organisation ethically and will keep the welfare of members in mind, but if not, you may end up paying to fund someone else with a nice wage for doing nothing.

As I said in the previous chapters, we as members have the power to mould the organisation, or at the very least to not agree with their processes and move on. If you think that there is something not right, investigate, observe, and if necessary, take action. It could be as easy as explaining to your instructor that you would like to know more about something or sending requests to officials with requests for transparency. It might be that your only option will be to leave. If the latter doesn't worry you too much then there are a lot of other organisations to try out. You will feel better once you find an organisation that is in line with your moral compass.

As a final story, I will share with you an account of my interaction with an organisation, discussing my mindset and actions at the time.

I contacted this organisation as on paper it looked amazing, focussing on the areas of training that I pursue. After a phone call I was promised funding for my own dojo, which would enable me to make an impact in my community and provide access to top courses. So, I duly signed up and paid my membership. I was promised a Gi, syllabus and all the legal documents and policies to run a dojo and I signed up for a coaching course. All looked great, till I started noticing that what was promised was not actually what was happening. We were promised a non-pressured environment with independence. The first thing I was faced with was "you cannot teach like that, you are a member of our organisation, you need to do as we do". Alarm bells had started to ring, but I decided to wait as my course papers were assessed.

Suddenly all of my emails were left without answer, the conversation about funding when quiet, and there was no mention about my dojo. No surprise there. They organised a tournament and I went with my students. I approached the head of the organisation and asked if I could start organising new classes using the coaching certificate number that I had been given as I had been told that we had passed. The head told me to wait as he was too busy right now. Fair enough, it was a busy tournament. During a break I was talking with one of my assessors about the same subject. I then saw the head storming towards me, so I turned and started to ask the same question again. I was faced with hostility, so I started to raise some other questions, all in a very respectful manner. The head nearly exploded and spat out shouting to me that if I don't stop asking questions, I will never see my qualifications, he will make my life hell, and I will never teach again. Well ok, I've heard these types of threats before, so I remained calm, although I was raging on the inside. I could not lose my temper as my students were listening to the conversation. What I was really disappointed about in this situation was the assessor, the second man in command. He could have taken action to sort this out, but he never did. He turned around and pretended not to be there. After the head had stormed off, I looked at the assessor with an expression of "wtf just happened?". He murmured a sorry and disappeared, like a genie. Well at least I knew what the organisation was about now.

I have to say that at the time I had received a phone call from a senior person in the UK warning me about the head of that organisation, which I'm very grateful for and I can proudly say that we have become friends and he is now my mentor.

On the way back my students told me that they were impressed by how calm I remained. I explained that I will not be disrespectful to anyone and clearly this guy has issues and needs help. Then I told my students that I'm no longer a member of this organisation but that if they would like to stay, I'd be happy to find them a club within that organisation. All three said that they did not want to be a part of organisations like that.

After my coaching documents arrived, I received a few messages from the head with congratulations and how it was great for me to wait to get them. I replied that I have moved on and am grateful for the course and qualifications, but that I don't want to be a part of it. There were no more threats as they really couldn't do anything in the first place.

So, as you can see, I followed the steps laid out in this book – been there, done that, got the t-shirt. I'm happy that I observed, analysed and asked questions that led to taking action. I tried to change things, but there was a lot of resistance, this is often what happens when one person is running the show. The best course of action was to move on.

Thank you for reading this book, please let me know what you think. Was it helpful? Did anything described in it relate to you or your experience? How have you dealt with organisations?

Some might ask why I haven't named and shamed the organisations that I have discussed. I know many people who have navigated the waters within those organisations and by association with me they may experience unpleasantries. As I outlined in my Think Positively section, I care about others and I don't wish to cause them problems. I'm also a firm believer that people need to experience their own life and learn. We can guide people, but they have to make decisions on their own. In all of the organisations that I described I'm not aware of any action taken by a student or organisation member that would constitute a crime. If that were the case then I would have reported them to the police / authorities.

Thank you for your support. I wish you all the best on your martial arts journey.

Kind regards,

Les Bubka.

About the Author

Les Bubka is a dedicated practitioner of the way of the empty hand and has been for over 25 years. He is the founder of Les Bubka Karate Jutsu, which incorporates the art of Karate with his personal training qualifications in order to help people.

Les has experience in running projects in association with mental health charities and other institutions, introducing Karate as a tool to help build confidence, self-esteem and physical activity to disadvantaged members of the community.

Les runs an inclusive club in Guildford (UK) where everyone is welcome.

Les is an established author, with his first book, Anxious Black Belt, being well received within the martial arts community.

For more information about Les Bubka and to connect with him directly please visit:

www.lesbubka.co.uk

Ready more by Les Bubka

Anxious Black Belt

Would you take up martial arts to fight anxiety?

"Strong and caring people are the pillars of society, and Karate helps to cultivate them." This is the maxim that Les has developed through his life journey. The Anxious Black Belt details the transformation of a happy child into a troubled teenager who discovered the benefits of the Japanese art of Karate, and his fight to overcome his anxiety. This is a light, fun and easy to read book that touches on the subject of mental health and how it has impacted the life of a young man who is trying to make sense of his feelings.

Thoughts On Karate: A Collection of Articles

Les Bubka's ever growing and changing insights on the Karate he teaches and trains in, and on the potential of the art as a whole. The diverse subjects chart not only Les' journey as a Karateka but also his development as a writer, expressing himself with ever greater clarity in a second language. From safe physical training to mental health, these eclectic articles are thought provoking and may challenge the preconceptions of many about how they approach their own discipline. Les does not ask or expect that you think along the same lines as him on every topic, but he does ask that you think.

Rules for Success in Karate

The rules detailed in this eBook have been compiled by Les Bubka based on the input from a variety of different authors that are well renown in the field of Karate. This eBook was created at the beginning of the COVID-19 pandemic as a way of inspiring those that may have found it difficult to remain optimistic and motivated in their training.

Please note that this eBook is available for free as a digital download. For further information please contact Les at info@lesbubka.co.uk.

Karate Journal

As a student of Karate, I was always encouraged to make notes about the training sessions and seminars that I attended, as well as my thoughts in general. Over the years I have used many different types of journals, from simple A5 notebooks and diaries through to dedicated martial arts books. They were always of great use to me, but none of them really provided the structure that I needed. That is why I have created this Karate for Mental Health (KFMH) Training Journal. This journal is designed to organise one's thoughts and observations, including training goals. You can argue that many other journals do the same, and you are right. However, one thing that was missing for me in my previous journals was the ability to track my mood before and after training. This would have allowed me to see how putting effort into training boosts my mental as well as physical well-being.

Printed in Great Britain
by Amazon